THE WOUNDED

Barbara T. Harrison

Copyright

All rights reserved. No part of this publication may be reproduced, distributed, or transmitted in any form or by any means, including photocopying, recording, or other electronic or mechanical methods, without the prior written permission of the publisher, except in the case of brief quotations embodied in critical reviews and certain other noncommercial uses permitted by copyright law.

Copyright © (Barbara T. Harrison), (2022).

Table of contents

CHAPTER ONE

As I opened my eyes to figure out where I was and who I was with, a light cigarette odor drifted over the room.

I carefully stood up from my resting position and draped a blanket over my bare body. I groaned as I realized where I was. I shifted my braided hair back to see the door open and a man enter.

"I've deposited the funds to your account, which you may check right now." The man's deep voice echoed around the room.

When I noticed an alert signal on my phone screen, I grabbed my phone to corroborate his story and nodded.

"A hundred and fifty thousand?" says the narrator. I sneered.

"Are you joking with me right now?" "Are you joking with me right now?" I also gave him death stares. "Didn't we agree on a number of 200?" "What exactly is this?" With a roll of the eyes, I inquired.

"Two hundred, certainly, but I was so inebriated last night that I couldn't remember the seeming pleasure we both shared." The man gave me a cold stare.

"I don't care if you were drunk, look, business is business," I said between clenched teeth, "so transfer the remaining fifty and I'll let this slip peacefully." He laughed.

"Are you currently threatening me, young lady?" The man barked, expecting me to quiver, but he had no idea that I was more than I appeared.

"Look, Miss Igraine, I've sent you the fifteen thousand dollars; take it or leave it; I don't mind. "

I got out of the bathroom, still wearing the blanket over my body, and walked into the room's bathroom. My clothes were laying on the bathroom floor, so I picked them up and put them on right away. I stepped out of the bathroom to see the obnoxious man on the bed smoking.

I stepped closer to the bed and grabbed my phone, then walked in front of the man and placed my phone in front of his face after opening my contacts.

"Doesn't this number right here belong to your wife?" I smirked, keeping a close eye on his countenance.

"What are you attempting to accomplish?" It isn't mine or my wife's!" The man yelled, and I could tell he was nervous, but he was still attempting to hide it.

"Okay, it doesn't belong to your wife," I said with a smile, "but what if I call her right now and ask her whether it actually belongs to your wife?"

"Look, if it's the $50,000 that's driving you crazy, then great, I'll send it to you right now, right here, and leave my wife out of it." The man was enraged. He then proceeded to make another cash transfer into my account.

"Now that's more like it," I thought as I saw the alert. Customers who are like this are simple to work with. He was too stupid to recognize that it wasn't his wife's phone number.

I walked out of the hotel room feeling as if my entire life was going to explode with joy.

Finally, I am financially secure enough to pursue a university education.

My name is Bridget, and I'd like to introduce myself. I'm a twenty-year-old girl who lost her parents five years ago in a fire, and after they died, I was forced to live with my auntie, who didn't seem to like me at all. I was recognized as being pretty, extremely pretty, everywhere I went. I was also known to be pretty and pleasant. People believe that if you're pretty, you have to be kind. Everywhere I went, people stared at me as if I'd just emerged from a cave full of diamonds; their stares were a little uncomfortable, but I'd become accustomed to it.

My auntie despised the fact that I was attractive, and she continually advised me not to let the concept of being attractive enter my mind. That isn't to say that beauty isn't important.

But she's completely wrong!

Everything revolves around beauty.

As my aunt tormented me, I recognized it wasn't right for me to be treated this way, and I knew I had to escape or I'd die in her hands one day. She's left so many scars on my body; she's ruining me, and I knew I had to leave.

I had no idea where to begin until one day. It was my last day of high school, and after finishing our school examinations, my friends and I decided to go out and have some fun, as some of our paths might be coming to an end at the end of the year. So one of Joy's friends told me that her aunt ran a pub and that we should all go there, and that's when my life changed. Mabel, her aunt, approached me and said she'd like to speak with me privately as soon as she saw me.

I accompanied her to a secluded area within the bar, where she immediately began congratulating me on my flawless, natural, and standard beauty. I remember my aunt telling me that I shouldn't let the concept of being beautiful deter me.

Believe me when I say that Joy's aunt Mabel seduced me with her comments, telling me that I shouldn't waste such beauty and should use it to make a living.

I wasn't sure what she meant at first; do individuals make money by having a pretty face? I was excited to learn how I could earn money with a gorgeous face, and I was focused on achieving only one goal. If I make enough money, my aunt's house will release me and I will be able to live independently without scars. My inquisitiveness and determination drove me to look for ways to generate money right now.

Aunt Mabel warned me not to tell any of my friends, including Joy, before she told me. One night, she confronted me, and I had to sneak out of the house while my aunt was deep asleep. Mabel brought me to a neighboring dress store, where she purchased a new one for me, and we both went to a party. That, I assumed, was the end of it. Attending parties, looking good, and making money

But then, at the party, a man in his late thirties approached us and smiled at Mabel.

Before taking my hand, the man murmured, "She sure is worth it."

I had no idea what was going on. With astonishment in my eyes, I stared at Mabel.

Mabel had told me, "It's going to be okay now, Faith." Why would she call me Faith if everything was going to be fine? What exactly was going on? As the man grinned and instructed me to stand up, I was terrified.

Mabel motioned me to stand up and told him to wait because I'd be there soon.

Where will I be in the near future? I was so terrified that I wanted to cry, and I had only recently turned eighteen. What exactly was going on?

Mabel urged me to take a deep breath since my name would be Faith that night and I'd have to amuse the man. I wasn't familiar with her brand of entertainment, and

When I entered the room where the man was, I saw him clad only in his boxers, and that's when I realized what was going on. I tried to flee the room, but the man caught me, and his voice resonated in my ear as his strong arms gripped my frail body. "I know it's your first time, and I know you're nervous, but I'd pay triple for a lovely girl like you, so don't be afraid; you'll have a great time."

At that point, my body felt like jelly, and my legs felt weak, and I collapsed to the ground. That night was so horrible that I dreaded remembering it, and the next thing I knew, I was crying in my bed. My virginity had come to an end.

Mabel tried to console me by claiming things would get better, and they did when Mabel asked if I wanted my money right then. I was taken aback. When I asked how much it cost, she claimed it was around $70,000. I made a lot of money in one night. I was upset about what had happened, but the money made me so happy that I forgot that my most valuable property had been snatched from me as if it were nothing.

I accepted the money from Mabel, but I had to receive it from her gradually so that my aunt did not become suspicious, which she did, and I had no choice but to flee. Mabel offered me her home, and I began living there. Every client I'd ever had never failed to compliment me on how attractive I was, and I was well aware of this...

I made more money than I could have imagined, and towards the end of the year, I had over 700,000 naira in my account. I'm so proud of you.

Mabel helped me in whatever way she could, and all I had to do was bring the money, and she happened to be a mother. An extremely young person who understands what it's like to be young

Two years had gone by, and I had never forgotten about my university, and I had begun to save money for it. I wrote the examinations, and not to seem arrogant, but I am quite intelligent. In all of my school papers, I was ranked first.

Two years of me enjoying my job and accumulating money for school and everything, culminating in my acceptance into one of the top universities I could find...

And now that I'm coming out of this hotel in broad daylight and dealing with con artists like this guy, I feel like I've spent all of my money on school.

As I waited for an Uber ride on a busy route, the city of Ohio became even more vivid. On Fridays, Ohio is always packed.

When I came home that morning, I went straight to the bathroom to take a warm bath.

I walked into the little living room with a towel wrapped around my body, to find Mabel carrying two suitcases.

Mabel inquired, "How was work today?"

"The idiot attempted to outwit me, but I was smarter," I said as I sat down.

Mabel said, "Now you know why you're Bridget." I grinned.

"So, what's up with the suitcase?" says the narrator. I inquired.

How do you manage to be so forgetful? Remember, you're going back to school on Monday? " Mabel looked at me with a raised brow.

"I understand, but isn't one suitcase enough?" With a shake of my head, I expressed my dissatisfaction with the situation.

"Is this one for your everyday clothes, and this one for your work clothes?" Mabel clarified.

"Work? I'm not allowed to work while I'm in school! " I sneered.

"Look Bridget, I have a lot of clients around here who are very wealthy and wouldn't want to lose out on someone like you; you can't afford to miss out on an opportunity like this," Mabel says, her lashes fluttering at me.

I let out a sigh. "fine"

"Wonderful," she said with a smile.

"You can take a break till you've completed your tasks." You must be exhausted; I'll assist you with packing. " Mabel gave a kind smile.

"Thank you, Mabel," I replied as I entered my room to change and sleep.

As I got into an Uber that Monday with my luggage and baggage in the back, I was both nervous and excited.

Mabel generated such a strong wave that it made me giggle.

The distance between my house and school felt like a thousand miles. Finally, I was relieved when I arrived at the hostel where I would be sleeping, which was about eight blocks from school.

So I was supposed to be living alone because I didn't want to share a room with anyone and cause any trouble, but the landlord pleaded with me, saying that students should help one another, and that's how I ended up having to stay with my new roommate, not because I didn't have enough money to rent the entire place, but because I was being nice. And she's been here for more than a week. It was rented a week ago, and I shall begin living there today.

After paying the Uber driver, I entered the building and dragged my two suitcases across the tiled floor to my room. I had to knock because the door was locked and it appeared to be from the inside.

When the door opened, I saw my roommate. And this is my first encounter with her. We've only communicated via social media, where she begged me to let us share a room.

"Hi, Bridget, you're here," she said cheerfully. Her lips appeared plumped, and her clothes and hair were rough.

Hmm.

"Yes, and are you Rose?" She nodded as I smiled.

As I entered the room, she appeared nervous, and why wouldn't she be? I saw a boy on her bed putting on his shirt.

That's the end of school for me. Now that I'm here, let's get back to business.

CHAPTER TWO

When I walked into my room, my roommate gave her male guest a warning look, and he immediately left.

After only a week, she's already inviting male friends over. She certainly is...

"Do you want me to assist you with unpacking?" Rose inquired, but I shook my head negatively.

I assured her, "Don't worry, I've got it under control," and she smiled.

Of course, our room was large, and I took up the majority of the space. Rose was quite content with the small space she occupied. I'm the landlady in our own room, so she has no say in the matter.

I unpacked everything and then made sure I got enough rest before thinking about anything else.

It was late at night when I received a phone call from Mabel. She asked how everything was, and I told her I'd unpacked and would start class the next day.

We both ended the call, and I quickly became bored.

Rose entered the room wearing a fancy gown and heels that made an ear-bursting noise as they collided with the tiled floor.

She appeared to have gone out.

She sat down on her bed and removed her shoes.

"Can I ask what course you're taking?"

I said right away, "Computer science."

"Oh, okay!" she exclaimed.

"You?" I turned to face her.

She replied, "Business administration."

"Are you a first-year student like me?" I inquired, and she nodded.

What, you're a freshman?

"Why do you feel like you've been here longer than a freshman?" I said as I looked at her dress.

When she realized what I meant, she laughed nervously.

"Oh, well, my friend hosted a birthday party, and besides, none of my friends are freshmen; they're all seniors," she explained, and I shrugged...

"Are you starting class tomorrow?" Rose inquired.

My gaze was drawn to her.

"Yes," I replied.

"OK, do you know your way around school or do you want me to assist you?" Rose grinned.

"That'd be fantastic; my first class begins at 1 pm," I said.

"Ohh... No, my first class starts at 12pm, so it looks like it'll be difficult. " Rose moved her head.

"It's fine, I can always ask around," I reassured.

"Oh no, I'm not going to let you ask around. Let me help. I have friends in the computer department as well. I'll tell one of them and let them know you'll need to know your way around the school, and besides, one of them can at least have the same time table as yours." Rose grinned.

I shrugged. "You don't have to make it a big deal."

"I do. You helped me out enough by letting me share a room with you. Let me at least help, even if it's in the smallest way," Rose said as I sighed.

"Sure, no problem."

"Good," she said, smiling.

I looked at my phone and went to my contacts; Mabel was the only one I had. To be honest, I've never had any pals. My call history was full of numbers from my clients, but my contact list was barren. I let out a sigh. It makes no difference whether you have friends or not. They're not going to change anything, and I like my life the way it is. peaceful and uncomplicated.

I put down my phone and crawled beneath my blankets, and the night flew by faster than I could have imagined.

It was the next day before I realized it.

When I awoke in my strange room, I heard a variety of sounds.

I turned around to see a swarm of pals gathered around Rose's bed... They all stopped talking when I sat up.

What? When did I become a remote control?

"Good morning!" says the speaker. I turned to Rose when I heard her voice and saw all of her pals staring at me. I'm used to being stared at.

I said, "Good morning."

There are three males and one female. With Rose bringing the number to five, it's no surprise that the room is already suffocating.

"As you must be Bridget, Rose told us about you," one of the girls said, and I nodded and rose.

I took my toiletries bag and exited the room, heading for the restroom.

Thanks to Rose and her pals, I was able to get dressed inside the bathroom after brushing my teeth and taking a bath.

When I returned to the room, Rose was still there with her pals.

Rose cried out, "So Bridget." "This is Sarah," she said, introducing the same girl.

"Hello," I said, as I waved at the girl.

"And just in case they aren't my other buddies, Emmanuel, Greg, Morris, and Austin," says the narrator. Rose continued, introducing her male companions.

It wasn't necessary for me to know.

So Sarah mentioned that she knows someone in the computer department as well; he's a freshman, and thankfully his timetable rhymes with yours, so instead of stressing yourself out, you can just go to class with him," Rose remarked, and I smiled...

"Thank you," I expressed my gratitude.

"It's not an issue," she added.

I returned to my bed and lay down till Rose's companions had left and Rose and I were alone. I got out of bed and sat up.

"Rose," I explained.

"Yeah," she says, almost too cheerfully at all times.

"So," I explained, "I'd want to chat about you and your buddies."

"How about them?" she inquired, removing her khaki shorts and replacing them with a pair of jeans.

I said, "I'd want to establish a rule in this room," I said, and she paused and turned to face me.

She inquired, "What rule?"

It's best not to invite too many people. It's making me suffocate. "I stated it clearly and unequivocally.

"Oh... "Sorry, I didn't realize it was suffocating," she murmured, rolling her eyes slightly, not realizing I had caught her.

"I'm not joking!" As I previously indicated,

"Okay, I got your message. But who knows, you might make too many friends to count, and letting them into the room implies you're breaching the rules as well "As mentioned by Rose.

"That is something I am aware of. I'm not stupid, but letting one friend in is fine, but two is too many, so..."

Rose said, "I understand, you're the boss," and mumbled the final phrases.

"All right, I'm heading to class a bit early." Rose replied as she snatched up her bag and a stack of books.

I didn't respond, and from the corner of my eyes, I noticed her flowering at me and rolled my eyes.

I sighed as she walked out of the room.

I wish I didn't have to share a room... This is why you should avoid sharing a room.

It's because this hostel is so close to school, and I could have hired another room or lived alone if the landlord hadn't pleaded so hard for Rose and me to stay together.

As Rose had departed, the room was tranquil and silent, and I realized it would soon be 1 p.m., so I decided to get everything ready for class.

A knock came at my door just as I finished.

I approached the door and opened it to see a very tall man standing there, his phone in his hand.

"Uh? Hello?" I drew his attention to myself.

"Did he lose his way or something?" He said, raising his eyes to reveal his thick brows and curly lashes.

"Is this room 002?" he inquired.

"Yeah, but why?" I retaliated.

He said, "I'm looking for a girl named Bridget."

"You're staring at her," I observed, and he paused for a moment before nodding.

He asked, "Oh, you're Bridget?" I nodded.

"Wow, a friend of mine told me you're experiencing problems at school and that you'd need someone to accompany you!" said the guy. "

I shrugged and said, "Well, it's okay. I advised her not to make a big deal out of it."

The guy shrugged and said, "Well, I'm already here."

"And why are you here so early when the class doesn't begin until one o'clock?" I began to look at the time on my table clock. It's only seven minutes after twelve o'clock.

I moaned. "I like to go to class early, settle in, and get prepared before the speaker takes over," the guy said, and I moaned.

"All right, come in. I'm still getting my books ready," I said as I opened the door for him.

I let him sit on my bed because there was no chair or anything around.

I prepared my books, put on my sandals, and grabbed my purse.

"All right, then,

We arrived at one of the four buildings in the school compound, and it was a monster.

"Now, lucky for us, we don't have to go all the way up the steps because our class is right here at the bottom of the building," the Guy remarked, pointing to our class's windows.

We both entered the classroom to find it vacant.

How did you get up so early?

The man took a step forward and laid his books on the long desk in the front seat.

Who in their right mind wants to sit in the front row?

"Are you not going to take a seat?" he inquired, his gaze falling on me and the empty space beside him.

"I don't think so. Front seats are not my favorite," I stated.

"Oh, well, I have really bad eyesight, and the lecturer's voice will be pretty clear from here, and you don't know how crowded this class gets," the guy stated, and I nodded.

I groaned and sat down next to him, slowly setting my books on the table.

It's strange to be in a class with just the two of us.

"So you just started school today?" the man inquired.

"Yes," I replied with a nod.

"Good," the guy continued, "you just have a little to catch up on. It's just a small introduction to COM101, and COM101 isn't that difficult. I heard it gets tougher when we get to COM103," I agreed.

He's got to be one of those smarty pants. I'm the same way.

Good...

"Do you mind if I scan through your books for a few minutes?" I muttered something, and he smiled and shook his head. "I wouldn't do that." You should also jot down some notes while scanning, "I nodded as he explained. "I will," says the speaker.

The guy hauled out a large textbook that shook the desk as I glanced at what they'd been studying for the past week.

He hesitated when I turned to him.

"I learn ahead of the instructor sometimes because it helps me comprehend more than I already do," the man added.

Wow, you're quite the nerd. And there was a time when I thought I was one of them.

He snatched his spectacles from his pocket and put them on.

Right. He stated that he had terrible vision.

We sat silent, studying, and time slowly passed us by. The glass began to fill up with people, and the speaker arrived an hour later, when the class had filled up.

I liked his lectures, and I thought it was amusing that he knew every answer to the lecturer's question but didn't bother to tell anyone, instead muttering it to himself. When I know an answer, I always raise my hand; I was rather popular in high school at the time.

My first class was over before we knew it, and by 3 p.m., my other class was beginning.

I inquired as the guy and I exited the classroom.

"How come you didn't answer any of the questions even though you knew the answers?"

He removed his glasses and chuckled awkwardly. He said, "I don't want to be noticed."

Oh.

I see. He's the type of guy that prefers to be alone.

"So," I explained, "I never got to know your name."

He said, "It's Clifford."

I said again, "Clifford."

Nice.

CHAPTER THREE

"So... I never learned your name." "It's Clifford," I said, and he replied, "Clifford."

Nice

"So, my next lesson starts at 3 p.m., and I'm looking forward to it."

"My class starts at 3 p.m. as well," I interrupted him.

"Wow, it looks like we've both got the same schedule." Anyway, I wanted to go get some lunch before my second session, because learning on an empty stomach is like watering a withered flower, "Clifford explained," and I almost grinned.

He needs to read a book about "how not to be a nerd."

"Well, I haven't eaten lunch either, so I imagine you won't mind if I join you for lunch?" "No, it's alright," he said, shaking his head. "There's a pretty huge canteen two blocks away from school, and their food is really great, you'll enjoy it." Clifford said something, and I nodded.

"So, what are we waiting for?" says the narrator. I smiled, and he began to lead the daisies.

Just two blocks away.

We entered the crowded canteen with a variety of delicious food aromas filling our nostrils and a variety of small chatter emanating from various tables.

Clifford and I were both seated at the same time, and the waitress took care of us right away.

We ordered the popular jollof rice, which looked to be the order of the day, and were promptly served.

"So, are you Rose's friend?" I inquired, initiating a dialogue. Both of us were far too silent "Who am I? Rose... I'm not sure who she is." Clifford answered.

"Huh? The girl who requested your assistance in getting to class today." As I previously indicated

"Oh, the girl who asked me to help you today is Sarah; I'm not familiar with this Rose you're talking about," Clifford responded.

Oh, okay, Sarah is Rose's friend, and I assume she is also Clifford's friend, although she has no idea who Rose is. Well, I understand friendship circles like that. "Sammy!" we both heard a voice, and a young man approached our table. He gave me a quick glance and smiled.

"Oh. Hey. George is a man with many talents "Clifford remarked

"I've been looking all around campus for you," George explained.

"Do you mind if I come along?" George inquired as he sat down. Why had he inquired in the first place?

Clifford looked at Kinglsey as he placed his order.

"Oh yeah, this is George, George meets Bridget," says the narrator. Clifford spoke first, and I forced a smile.

"Hello, Bridget." George flashed one of his most charming smiles. As he smiled, his not so-deep dimple produced a promising hole on both sides of his cheeks, and you could tell it was one of his best. "Hi," I said.

The three of us ate quietly as George's dinner was brought to the table.

Until Clifford and George started a conversation of their own.

"Have you seen Rita, by the way?" George enquired.

"No, and you know how she is; one minute she's in school, the next minute she's in another country," Clifford remarked, casting a sidelong glance at me. I stood up and raised my hand.

"Another country?" you might wonder. "I'm simply exaggerating so you'll understand how her body and legs would never be at rest and stay in one place," George said again. "You're right," Clifford added. George chuckled.

The three of us had finished our lunch and were walking out of the canteen when we heard a loud "Guys" behind us, causing us to turn around. I had no idea why I had turned. I'm not acquainted with anyone.

Clifford was hugged by a thin female about my height with pale skin and braided hair who walked up to the males.

"Oh Rita," Sammy replied, his face indicating that he wanted out of the hug.

"Oh my God, Sammy, it's been a long time since I've seen you," she said with a smile.

Clifford said, "You saw me last night."

"I realize it's been a long time, but where did you shout this morning?" We were both on our way to class when you abruptly vanished. " "Joyce called," George told her. Rita said, "She asked me to give her some stuff."

"Something?"

"However, who is this?" Rita shifted her gaze to me.

"Hello, my name is Bridget." I mentioned earlier that Clifford may open another introductory center.

"Nice to meet you. My name is Rita," she said with a smile.

"So, where are you going, guys?" Rita enquired.

"Class," Clifford answered.

"I'm going to take a nap now that my classes are finished for the day," Clifford said.

"Would you like to hang out with me now that my classes are out for the day?" George shrugged when Rita inquired.

"Anyway," Clifford said as he turned to face me, "Let's go," he continued, and I shrugged and followed him.

The day went by slowly as usual, and I returned to my hostel just after my second lesson concluded. Clifford, on the other hand, went... wherever. I'm still grateful for how he assisted me today. And it's funny how he made me a sloppily drawn yet attractive and clear map of the school to help me prepare for my next lesson the next day, because he claimed it's not every day he'll be helpful.

I climbed into bed and checked the clock; it was 5:30 p.m. Rose hadn't returned yet, so it was just me in the room when Mabel called.

"Hey," I said.

"Alright, I see. Have you made any friends? " Mabel was the one who inquired.

Have I done so?

I met Clifford, George, and Rita today, for example. But, on the other hand, is knowing each other's names considered establishing friends? I don't know. I didn't have much time after high school to develop pals. I had become accustomed to being alone. I'd be napping if I wasn't 'working' or didn't have any work to do that day.

I said into the phone, "No, I didn't."

"Make friends, have fun, go to parties, and stay out late. You'll grow old if you don't have as much fun as I do, "Mabel cracks jokes."

"I'm having a good time laying in bed." I chuckled.

Mabel stated, "I know you're not."

Of course, I'm Bridget; I know how to have a good time; I know how to stay out late, even sneak out; I know how to make friends; I know how to get a thousand boyfriends; but no, let me adjust to this place first; I'm already hating my roommate, and I want to focus more on my books; that will be great," I stated.

"Oh yeah, I forgot you're those geeks who spend their lives engrossed in literature; I came across your old report cards once, and goodness, your grades are on fire," Mabel exclaimed dramatically.

I burst out laughing.

She's referring to me as a nerd. Then she should meet Clifford. "I'm sorry, Mabel, but I have to leave; I'll call you later." I'm tired of being awake, "I muttered this as I slammed the door shut. And then I fell asleep with my phone against my face.

The next morning, I awoke unusually early since I had slept far too long the night before.

The door clicked open at 7 a.m., and Rose strolled in wearing a revealing outfit.

"Good morning," she said with a smile.

I said, "Good morning."

Is she just getting back from somewhere?

That suggests she didn't return home the night before.

I got ready right away because my class started at eight o'clock. She should go and return.

I put on a pair of sandals and grabbed my large purse, dressed in a cropped sweater and loose pants. I glanced at Rose, who was deep asleep on her bed. How precise.

When I moved back to find Clifford standing in front of the door, his palm up in a fist, I grabbed the room key and opened the door to go out.

Was he preparing to ring the doorbell?

"Clifford?" I dialed the number. I lock the door and head outside.

I inquired, "What are you doing here?"

"Uh," he said hesitantly, before returning his gaze to me. "I was terrified."

"Afraid?" I slant my head, allowing him to see my perplexed expression.

"I drew you a map of the school, but I was worried you wouldn't get it."

What a lovely gesture.

I shrugged. "I completely understand it." "My first lesson today is on the third floor of the school's second building, in the fifth classroom; your map wasn't particularly detailed, but it was understandable, and I like it."

Well, I'm glad I could help; I was too preoccupied with the bad aspects of today, thinking about what might happen if Bridget doesn't comprehend the map and misses class, so that's why I came here.

I smiled at how thoughtful he was towards a girl he had just met.

"Thank you," I said with a smile.

"No problem," he said, "would you like to attend class with me now that I'm here?"

What's to stop you?

We both walked out of the hostel and noticed a girl approaching us. Our path was abruptly stopped by her.

"Sorry" she said to me and turned to Clifford.

"Sammy!" "Please, just for today," she requested.

"Great, can you make it by 1pm?" the girl asked, and Clifford replied, "I'm not sure I can."

"Sammy, please na," the girl said, a fake frown on her face and a sorrowful expression on her face.

"All right, but only today," Clifford responded, and the girl grinned.

"Do you want me to come to your place or..."

"I'll pay you a visit." Clifford remarked.

Clifford smiled and nodded.

"Thanks, Sam," she remarked cheerfully as she walked into the hostel from which we had just emerged.

I didn't want to pry, but I've always been inquisitive, so why should I now?

"Who is she?" says the narrator. Clifford was the one who asked.

Clifford said, "Oh, that's Success; she's George's friend," and I nodded.

"And what was she pleading for?" says the narrator. I inquired. How did I become such an inquisitive creature?

"I frequently assist her with her homework. And it appears that I'll be assisting her once more today. "Clifford shrugged his shoulders.

"Do you get paid?" asks the narrator. I inquired.

"Why should I be compensated?" Clifford made a snide remark.

"What? It is not free when people do something for others; no matter where I go or what I see, nothing is free; haven't you heard that life is a give-and-take situation? " I let out a gasp.

"Can't I just give without taking?" I mean, it's just assignments; I do it all the time for different individuals, and their 'thank you' is enough for me.

"So when people ask you to do something for them, you do it for them for free." I was on the verge of yelling.

I don't see anything wrong with it, and I'm not in any financial need; I'm financially secure, and getting paid with something like that would make me appear greedy, so I'm simply being helpful. Clifford smiled and nodded.

How is he the most thoughtful person I've ever encountered in my twenty years of life? No one I know, and I mean no one, is as nice as him.

"All well, then," I said, shrugging.

We both arrived at class that morning, and I couldn't stop thinking about how serious Clifford looked in his spectacles, and how gorgeous he looked.

The speaker rushed through the session; we were meant to finish by 10 a.m., but he finished by 9 a.m., leaving us with a difficult task that enraged the class.

Students began to leave the room, but Clifford remained seated and began working on his duties. Already!

"You have plenty of time; our next class isn't until 2:00." "So you've got a lot of time to work on your project," I explained.

Well, I share a room with George, who isn't really I'm at a loss for words... Just keep in mind that you won't be able to study or read with him in the room with you. He plays to ear bursting if he doesn't have any pals over.

Like Rose, for example.

"If he does things that you don't like, tell him that you don't like them; you're both paying the rent, and you have a say in whether or not you like him having friends over or him playing music," I continued, motioning Clifford to remove his spectacles.

"If I wanted to, I could tell him." But that would be impolite.

"I don't see anything impolite there; you're just being human," I began.

"Well, I'll tell him eventually," says the narrator. Clifford shrugged his shoulders.

Someday?

What type of dude is he?

"You're simply being human," I began to argue.

"Well, I'll tell him eventually," says the narrator. Clifford shrugged his shoulders.

Someday?

What type of dude is he?

CHAPTER FOUR

Clifford is the most naive person I've ever met. I'm not trying to be disrespectful or insult him, but he is the most naive person I've ever met. It's endearing that he's a thoughtful human being who is also helpful and pleasant. But his naivety is making me think of him as a naïve individual. It's just in his character; some individuals are born polite.

It's far too lovely. Or maybe I'm just too naive...

I sat in silence as he worked on his project; I didn't even want to finish mine because I had plenty of time and planned to do it at home.

I jumped up and collected my suitcase as I realized we'd be going our separate ways after this class. I should depart ahead of time.

Clifford abruptly inquired, "Where are you going?"

"Back

"All right, see you in the next class," I said, handing him the entire classroom.

I felt like I was going to pass out as I stepped out of the building; the building stairs were to die for. I was short of breath and coughed after swallowing my own spittle. "Bridget?" I wondered.

I heard a voice and wanted to glance up to see who it was, but my cough was getting worse.

"Are you all right, Bridget?" the voice said.

Evidently, I'm not.

"I hope you don't mind, but here take this," the speaker said, and I looked up to see George... I'm being handed a bottle of water.

I snatched it from him, flung the cover aside, and drank the water slowly. My throat finally cleared, and I exhaled a sigh of relief, saying, "Thank you."

"You're welcome," he added, "but don't hurt yourself."

I explained, "I wasn't aiming to hurt myself; in the first place, this staircase did a fantastic job."

"It'll become second nature to you." George gave a warm grin.

"Thanks," I said, nodding.

"Are you going to class?" he inquired.

"Actually, I'm returning to the hostel because my lesson just ended," I explained.

"Would you like to walk with me?" He gave a friendly smile.

Hmm.

"Clifford, on the other hand, is still in class; I heard you two remain together, so you can wait for him instead." I tried to be courteous.

"Oh Clifford knows his way back, you're the newcomer here," George said, "just so you don't miss your home."

"Uh... I believe I'm familiar with this area... Also, just so you know, I have a map with me "As I already indicated.

George regarded me with skepticism.

"All right, can we just stroll back together?" says the narrator.

"Sure," I replied.

We strolled to my hostel without saying anything because whenever he starts a conversation, it ends almost as soon as he starts it. Perhaps I'm just not in the mood to continue.

I was hungry and tired.

Instead of stating he wanted to walk with me, he should have said he wanted to walk with me.

He stopped walking as soon as we arrived at the building where I live.

"All right, now that you're home, I'll leave," he said.

"Thank you very much," I added.

"It's not nothing," he said with a smile and a slight wave as he walked away.

When I entered my room, Rose was fast asleep on her bed. My next lesson is at 11:30 p.m., so I just have an hour.

I was able to eat, but I was unable to rest because time was not on my side.

In irritation, I gathered my books for class and walked to class, knowing where my next class was thanks to Clifford's map.

Surprisingly, when I arrived at class, it had already begun to fill up with kids, and I noticed Clifford sitting on the front row. I grinned to myself as I saw him adjust his spectacles and arrange his books in a nice manner. I wanted to sit next to him, but a woman sat next to him, beaming her heart out.

I shrugged and took a seat near the rear of the class, near the window.

The professor began to speak, and Clifford was correct; it was difficult to understand what he was saying. I did my best to concentrate, and I was successful.

I didn't catch the complete lecture at that time because I was spacing out a lot; nevertheless, I had no idea why I was spacing out. Despite the fact that I had nothing on my mind, I did.

The lesson concluded, and I believe the professor mentioned something about next week and a project due soon.

Isn't it too early to start planning projects?

As I packed my books, my gaze was drawn to Clifford, who appeared to be having an animated conversation with the girl seated next to him, the girl laughing and sticking her tongue out like a goat.

Ugh.

Clifford paused in his conversation with the girl and began gazing about, as if looking for someone.

I kept my sight fixed on him, and as his head rotated to look in my direction, he recognized me and smiled and waved.

I averted my gaze and put down my bag.

He snatched his luggage and dashed up to me.

"Hello, I was worried you wouldn't make it to class." He was a little out of breath when he said it.

"Why wouldn't I?" says the narrator. I inquired, my gaze falling on the girl whose glance was hurting me. That's right, the same girl that sat next to Clifford.

"My map isn't particularly detailed. Did it make a difference?" Clifford had inquired.

"I wouldn't be here right now if it didn't." I came back with a response...

"It's all right. Anyway, your girlfriend appears to be on the verge of murdering me, so I'm heading back to my hostel. I'm exhausted." As I have indicated.

"Is she my girlfriend?" Clifford's eyes expanded and his face remained blank.

I pointed to the female he was seated with earlier, slowly and elegantly.

"Funny, Daniella is simply a buddy of mine," Clifford said as he turned away from her.

"Are you certain? I'm not fond of the way she was staring at me "I went on to say.

"Yes, I am certain. She's merely a friend I met through George two weeks ago "Clifford remarked.

I looked at Daniella, and her eyes were definitely catching my attention.

"All right, Clifford, pretend you're looking for someone and slowly glance at her to see her glaring at me," I said, and Clifford looked perplexed.

Clifford Daniella was shooting me death glares as I slowly turned around.

He abruptly returned my gaze.

He apologized, "I'm sorry."

I scoffed, "You shouldn't be."

"She's giving you those eyes because of me," Clifford explained, "so I should at least apologize."

How adorable.

"Are you certain she doesn't like you or anything, because I don't like being in the middle of things, and she doesn't either."I inquired, my head cocked.

"I don't know," Clifford said, looking sideways.

I said, "You wouldn't."

"Anyway, I'll be gone until tomorrow," I explained.

"I'm actually... I'm heading to your hostel as well." Clifford spoke quickly.

"Really?" I cocked my head to look at him.

"I've assured Success that I'll assist her with her assignment." Clifford elaborates.

Oh, that's right, the girl from earlier in the day.

"All right, then, we'll go together." I just shrugged.

Clifford and I were walking back to the hostel, which was not far from the university, and we were both quiet and enjoying the walk.

I wouldn't say I loved it, so I felt compelled to speak up, but I couldn't think of anything, so I remained silent.

It's not like we're strangers; I met him the day before yesterday, and we're only half strangers. I don't know much about him, but I can tell he's a pretty nice guy.

When I arrived at my hostel, I simply bid my goodbyes to him as he made his way to the success room. Wow.

How did I become so uninteresting?

I walked into my room and shut the door behind me. Rose was on the bed, talking on her phone with her friend Sarah.

I want to live on my own.

"You're back," Rose said, smiling as I slid my suitcase next to my bed.

"Yes!" I exclaimed.

"So, I baked some sweet potatoes and fried eggs, and I left some for you as well!" As expressed by Rose.

Really?

She's attempting to win my favor.

That's really nice. I don't believe I have a redeeming quality.

Nonetheless... It's all about the food in this case. I don't mess around with food.

"Thank you," I told her.

"You're welcome," she said with a smile as she turned to face her pal.

I exhaled a sigh of relief as I yanked my tiny pants off my body. I changed into a more comfortable outfit and didn't waste any time eating into the sweet potatoes and eggs.

"Are you going?" says the narrator. Sarah said something to me.

"Of course I am; after all, who would want to miss such a party?" Rose went on to say.

Sarah added, "Asin." "However, John will be there; are you certain you'll be fine?"

"Who the hell is John, that moron?" Rose said with a sigh and a roll of her eyes.

From my bed, I observed the two females talking about boys and stuff before returning to the party they were talking about earlier.

They both saw I was watching them, and Rose turned to face me.

"So, Bridget... On Friday, there's still a party going on, and...

"I'm not going!" exclaims the speaker. I cut her off with a shake of my head.

Rose grumbled bitterly, "Wow, you didn't let me finish." "May I inquire as to why?" she inquired.

Please don't misunderstand what I'm saying. I'm a party animal who enjoys going to parties with people my age, but going to parties with people you don't know is a another story. Even though I go to parties with a lot of strangers, I still go to meet people with whom I want to do business. It's as if I need a car to go to parties. As if there was a reason for it. I'm not sure. It's just that it's difficult. I'm a conundrum.

I told Rose, "Parties aren't my thing."

"Well, it's one of the first parties for freshmen like us, and it's on a Friday night, the day after tomorrow. Seriously, you don't want to miss it." Sarah

I said, "well... I'll think about it."

"Will you think about it or will you say no?" Rose smirked.

"What makes you so desperate for me to come?" I grumbled.

"For one, you're attractive, and you appear to be an eye-catcher."

Why does she sound as if she wants to brag about me at the party?

"And two," Rose said, "the entire hostel will be silent because everyone is attending, so you'll be the only one alone."

And if she goes to the party, I'll have the room to myself; who cares if the hostel is empty.

"Well," I admitted, "I'm still thinking about it."

"All right, just give me your feedback tomorrow or whenever you like, but before the party," Rose said, and I agreed.

It's a definite 'No,' because I have a class at 4 p.m. and still have time to recover. Yay.

We all heard a knock on the door, and I had to go get it because my bed was closer to it. It's not like I know somebody who would go out of their way to find me and knock on my door.

When I opened the door, Clifford appeared unexpectedly.

I yelled out, "Clifford."

"Hello," he said with a smile.

"What exactly are you up to...

I took a breather since I remembered exactly what he was up to. Assisting a young lady named Success.

"How did the assignment go?" I inquired.

"It was a little difficult.

I was leaving, and I wanted to come say hello or goodbye before leaving. I couldn't think of anything to say. Clifford elaborates.

"It's absolutely a hello," I said, "since we'll probably see each other again by 4 p.m."

"Well, that's terrific. Well, then good bye," Clifford remarked as he walked away.

Because of Sarah and Rose's stares, I almost slipped and collapsed as I shut the door.

"Was that Sammy?" Sarah was the one who inquired.

I gave a nod.

"Since when have you and he gotten so close that he had to come over and say 'hi'?" Rose asked, smiling. "I seldom talk to him even though I know him."

Sarah said, "Well, I'll be right back," and walked out of the room.

I shrugged and returned to my bed to finish my meal.

She has to be aware.

I told Rose, "You're a really good cook."

"Thank you," she said with a smile.

CHAPTER FIVE

I awoke to the sound of my ear-piercing alarm tone, which I had set up hours before falling asleep.

I put on my slim pants and a black blouse, slipped on my sandals, and took my bag.

Rose and Sarah were no longer in the room. While I was still sound asleep, all they spoke about was the Friday party. Ugh.

With my books in hand, I headed out of the hostel and into class. We've already completed com104, and I don't believe computer science is a difficult subject.

I arrived at class, and this time I made sure I sat in the front row, as the rear sitters were doing OK. They're putting in a valiant effort. How do they manage in such a vast group?

I grinned to myself when I noticed Clifford's books neatly set on the desk in front of an empty chair, surprised that he wasn't in class. He's always early, of course. What a "Clifford" character he is.

I looked around the classroom to see if you'd seen him, and I noticed him walking inside. He was stopped at the door by a young child, and the two of them began to converse.

They were so far away that you couldn't hear a thing, save from the noises from other pupils in the room.

Clifford's face brightened up, and his smile was gorgeous, to be honest. Clifford and the youngster appeared to be on good terms.

"Is he all right?" I turned to see a girl after hearing someone beside me. Her lips were plumped and filled, and her eyes were as brilliant and shiny as ever, despite her dark skin.

"What?" I shrugged at her.

She grinned as she said, "You've been staring at Sammy for the past ten seconds."

What is this person's name again?

Oh, my gosh.

"And for the previous 10 seconds, you've been staring at me staring at Clifford?" She chuckled when I asked.

"Anyway, my name is Mary," she said with a smile.

"I didn't inquire about your name." As I previously stated In certain ways, she wouldn't consider me impolite.

"I was only being friendly," she explained.

"All right, my name is Bridget," I said.

But, honestly, Sammy is incredibly attractive; I mean, he's just a freshman like us, but I see some seniors staring at him with lustful eyes.!" Mary spoke up, her gaze fixed on Clifford's way.

"And I saw you look at him with sexual eyes as well," I said, to which she laughed.

"You do as well!" she responded.

"Think whatever comes to mind." I just shrugged.

"Anyway, it's true that I like Sammy; who doesn't? He's brilliant, friendly, and insanely wealthy." Also, don't forget about his attractiveness. "However, despite having all of those traits, I feel him to be quite confined and tight, as well as an introverted type of guy that doesn't seem to fit into any social status," Mary added.

"Excuse me, but why are you telling me this?" I pressed my face against hers.

How did a parrot become so easily freed out of its cage?

"I'm not sure, I just thought it'd be something you'd like to hear, and plus, I'm just trying to warn you about Sarah, that fly is constantly hovering around him, do you know what I'm talking about?"

I'm sorry, but I don't, and I'd appreciate it if you could just leave me alone... Thank you... Please" As I already indicated,

This conversation is disgusting and immature to me.

She stormed away enraged, rolling her eyes.

The professor entered the room, and Clifford took his seat next to mine.

"Hello," he said with a smile.

"Hello," I said, directing your attention to my books.

Clifford took his spectacles out of his bag and put them on.

This is one of those things that never gets old.

By 6 p.m., class was over, and Clifford and I were walking out together.

"Did you hear this morning that we'll be working on a project next week?" As we made our way down the stairwell, Clifford inquired.

"Yes, I was in the back and didn't get any information, but yes, of course, I checked the scheme and we should have a project because we're already in com104," I explained.

"Did you check the schemes as well?"

"Who doesn't?" says the narrator. With a shake of my head, I expressed my dissatisfaction with the situation.

All right, and we'll be doing a database project in groups, and the instructor mentioned we get to choose our group mates, so I was wondering if you'd like to be in mine." Clifford had inquired.

"You already have a group," I said, as I turned to face him.

"Yes, about five individuals approached me this afternoon requesting to be in the same group as me, but I only chose two people and saved a seat for you," Clifford said with a smile.

How thoughtful of you.

And, of course, who wouldn't want to be a part of Clifford's group when he's this smart?

I turned to face him as we exited the building.

"You understand that people want to be on your side just because you're clever." I informed him.

He replied, "Yes, I know."

"They want to be able to rely on a smart person to work on the project." I also added...

He said, "Yes, I'm aware of it."

"They want to take advantage of you," I explained.

He said, "I know."

"And you don't give a damn?" I was on the verge of yelling.

"I don't consider it to be a negative or..." It's all right. "He smiled and nodded.

This guy is serious.

"Are you going to be in my group?" he inquired.

"Yes, and no matter what, I'll make sure I use you." I cracked a joke, and he laughed.

He shrugged and said, "Go ahead."

I said, "I'm joking. I despise relying on others; you'll get nothing in return, so just trust yourself."

We both fell silent once more. I despise being alone, so I started with a silly one.

"Did you hear anything about the Friday night party?" I inquired.

What was I thinking...

Clifford sighed, "Oh that."

Oh well, he's aware of it. I'm taken aback.

"Are you aware of that as well?" I inquired.

Clifford smiled as he said, "George won't shut speaking about it."

"And Rose as well," I groaned.

"And it appears that the entire world is watching," I scoffed.

Clifford answered, "Yes, including me."

Wait...

"Really?" I gave him an odd look.

Don't laugh, but this will be my first time attending a party. And I'm being pushed to go because I don't enjoy crowds or gatherings. I despise crowded situations. "He said it all at once.

That's how an introvert communicates. Clifford, as well as the way I see him. He is essentially an introvert who aspires to be an extrovert but is unable to do so.

"Oh, I see," I shrugged, "but I do go to a lot of parties."

"You're going to this one, right?" Clifford's face was glowing brightly.

"No!" exclaims the speaker. I sneered.

"Why?" he inquired.

"There's no rationale for it. Simply put, no "I just shrugged.

"And you don't want to go because you're being forced to, right? Who is forcing you?" I inquired.

He burst out laughing. "George."

"Just say no," I advised.

"I did," Clifford explained, "but then he said if I come, I can ask him for anything or any favors, and truly, this is an opportunity to respectfully beg him to stop playing those songs."

I came to a halt.

"No, it doesn't have to be an occasion for you to tell him what you're entitled to, such as asking him to stop playing or refrain from doing something you dislike. You must master the art of saying no "With a shake of my head, I expressed my dissatisfaction with the situation.

"No," he responded emphatically. He laughed, "There, I said it."

"It's not funny, honestly, just tell him, and then say no to the party, it's that simple," I added, as we both resumed our stroll.

"It may appear simple to you, but rejecting someone down makes me feel so horrible that I begin to despise myself for it, and trust me, that feeling is the worst."

With a shake of my head, I expressed my dissatisfaction with the situation. Clifford is about to break my heart.

"Look, in this world, one must be crafty and wicked, according to Leo Tolstoy." As I have indicated.

"Huh?" Clifford shifted his gaze to me. "Do you want me to turn evil?" "I'm not sure what you're talking about!"

"I'm not suggesting you should be wicked, but we live in a terrible world. Get good, but don't reveal it all at once or you'll be trampled." You could think I'm giving you poor advise or something, but you don't want to be a deer in a lion's den," I explain, and he smiles.

"I see what you're getting at."

"You're giving me tips on being evil, but you don't appear to be wicked or rude," Clifford observed.

"It's because I'm a jerk."

"Good... So everyone has good and terrible qualities, and that's what I'm trying to say, and I'm suggesting you let out the— "Sammy!" We both turned around when we heard Clifford's name from behind us.

"As well as Bridget." As soon as we turned around, George smiled.

"Hello," I said courteously.

"It's strange how I constantly envision you two together," George said with a smile.

"It's not strange that we're on the same schedule," Clifford explained.

"So, do you mind if I join you?" George was the one who inquired.

He has a habit of asking if he may continue doing what he's doing.

Clifford said, "Sure."

We strolled together, with me in the middle, and were completely silent.

We walked quietly the entire way, and I saw the boys weren't going their way, but rather my way.

"Are you on your way home?" I inquired of the two youngsters who were pointing in the opposite direction.

George answered, "Well, I'm meeting someone near your hostel."

"How do you feel, Clifford?" I inquired.

He said, "I'm walking you home."

Wow. I'm sure he's a trustworthy individual.

"Thank you," I answered.

When we arrived at the hostel, I wished Rose had prepared something ahead of time once more. I was famished.

I said to each of the boys, "Thank you very much."

"It's nothing!" exclaims the speaker. George remarked. "It's time for me to get on the road; there's still a little but a long way to go."

"George, Clifford has something to say to you before you leave!" I remarked hastily.

I'm not sure why I'm doing this; perhaps it's because it's troubling me too much.

"Do I?" Clifford gave me a surprised expression.

I looked at him and said, "Yes, you do."

Clifford was undoubtedly perplexed as George gazed back and forth at me. Clifford is perplexed as well.

I sighed and opened the bag to let the fluid out.

"Clifford says he despises it when you have too many people around and play loud music; it doesn't give him enough room or time to study; the last time he did his homework in class..." I go on and on about how I clutch the books in my hands...

Clifford fixed his gaze on me. His pupil had blown out entirely.

George gave a brief glance at Clifford before returning his gaze to me.

Okay, I'm not surprised this is coming from you and not from Sammy, because he doesn't let anyone know how he feels, and OK, if you have any issues with me, just tell me and don't worry, I'll turn off the ear-piercing music and invite no one. Clifford received a glance from George.

I'm not suggesting you don't invite people around... They shouldn't be excessive. " Clifford remarked.

"All well," George shrugged. "And next time, just tell me what you don't like and don't make a girl do it instead," George said and gave a mocking smile.

Clifford sighed and said, "I understand."

Before walking away, George flashed me one more dimpled smile.

Clifford sighed deeply. "You know, you didn't have to do that."

I admitted, "I did."

"I was planning on telling him after the party, which would have been less impolite." Clifford was the one who responded.

"No, this approach wasn't disrespectful either, and George clearly grasped the situation. Everyone knows you're an introvert, and don't worry, you're free to study at home now, and you're not even required to attend the party," I explained, and Clifford smiled.

"Thank you," he responded abruptly.

I grinned.

"Thank you very much."

"Anyway, I'll see you tomorrow," I remarked as I proceeded inside the building, where I accidentally collided into Sarah, or she accidentally bumped into me.

She promptly apologized, "Sorry."

"It's fine," I said.

I strolled past her on my way to my room.

CHAPTER SIX

I strolled past Sarah and into my room, passing along the corridor. She must have come to see Rose.

When I entered the room, I discovered Rose reading and eating on her bed.

"You're back," she said with a smile.

"Yes," I responded, emphasizing the "s" and tossing my luggage onto my bed.

"All well, so I made supper and Dec...

I grinned.

That's exactly what I needed to hear.

If Rose is attempting to win my favor, she should just keep cooking. She'll quickly win me over.

That evening, I felt like I was going to burst since I despised the entire dinner.

I chose to start on my homework yesterday, and after attempting it, I was finished in no time, so I decided to study databases more in preparation for our project next week.

I dozed off while studying, and that was the end of my day.

The next day, I awoke feeling... well, the same, not joyful, unhappy, stressed, or energized. I was nothing but a...

I'm not sure.

I got out of bed and went to the bathroom to take a bath. Apparently, we have four classes today, and thank goodness it's Friday, when we just have two classes.

We were on time for class at 7:00 a.m., and I was running late. I found myself sprinting in my short Jean skirt, which was plastered to my thighs like it would never come off.

When I arrived at class and realized I'd have to sit in the back, I sighed when I noticed Clifford in the front seat. Extremely responsible.

I took off like an aircraft as soon as class ended.

When I got home, I decided to get some sleep in preparation for the next lesson. I'm not sure how I'm getting so tired so rapidly these days.

I attended the three sessions that afternoon without really meeting Clifford, for two reasons: one, I was too weary; and two, I was late for every class and had to sit in the back; and I departed as soon as class was finished.

I felt like I was going to pass out in the last class of the day. What is it that makes me so exhausted, not just tired but sleepy? Is it just my lazy side kicking in, or did I get enough rest for today? I was asleep in class, and trust me when I say that this is the first time I've ever dozed in a class; I've never dozed in a class before, from elementary school through secondary school.

The professor was so far away, and his voice sounded like a hypnotist trying to hypnotize his patient to fall asleep with his voice.

I looked at the clock and it was exactly 5 p.m. I used to be like that.

And with that, I was fast asleep.

I sat properly and sighed as my eyes fluttered open. I looked to my side to see Clifford sitting opposite me, his spectacles occupying his eyes and his books occupying his attention.

I looked around the classroom and noticed that it was completely empty.

It had also become cloudy, so I took out my phone and checked the time.

"6:06pm," I noted.

Clifford removed his spectacles and placed them in their case, saying, "So you're finally awake."

"Yes, but wait. What went wrong? " I was perplexed because I was aware that I had slept off during the previous period and that Clifford was seated in the front row.

"I discovered you fast asleep and in a kind of deep sleep after class, and I didn't want to wake you up, but I couldn't leave you alone in class, so I stayed and waited until you woke up on your own." Clifford elucidated Gosh.

"Th..thanks?" I looked perplexed.

So, instead of going home to relax, he stayed here to watch me sleep.

"You could have woken me up instead, and then gone home early and gotten some rest. It's getting late now, and it'll be dark soon "I let out a sigh.

He shrugged and said, "It's fine."

I got to my feet and grabbed my luggage.

"It isn't, but thanks anyhow; may we leave now?" I inquired, and he nodded.

I strolled into my empty room, pondering Rose's whereabouts. Perhaps she's in the company of Sarah.

I groaned and climbed into bed for a second round of sleep.

When I awoke the next morning, I was overjoyed. Today is Friday, and we only have two courses, one at 12 p.m. and the other at 3 p.m. What a delight!

Unlike Rose, who was happy and holding her phone, I spent my time reading.

She does, however, have pals with whom she speaks on the phone. Mabel is the only one I have.

How depressing.

I laughed out loud and went back to reading.

Rose had prepared breakfast for us that morning, and I was overjoyed, so I inquired while eating.

"Rose, let's make a deal: I'll give you the money for food here every day, and all you have to do is cook; you set the price, and I'll decrease it; all you have to do is cook. What do you think?"

I'm a slacker when it comes to cooking, but Rose enjoys it and is quite good at it. So this deal seemed to be too good for her to pass up.

"Deal," she said with a smile.

I see we've finally reached an agreement on one phrase.

I noticed Sarah and Clifford walking towards the building as I slipped on a Jean short, a stretchy body-hugging shirt, and some black sandals to get ready for class that afternoon.

They both came to a halt when they saw me.

Clifford gave a kind smile.

"Bridget," Sarah said, a smile on her face.

She's acting as though we've known each other for a long time. Okay, Well...

I responded, a slight smile on my face.

Clifford remarked, "You're early."

I said, "Yes, I am."

I won't be able to sit at the back today.

"I came here specifically for you so that we could go together," Clifford explained.

"I believe you stated that you wanted to assist someone with an assignment." Sarah added her two cents.

"The guy I was supposed to help said he doesn't have any spare time today, so it'll have to wait until tomorrow," Clifford explained.

Wow.

"Can you tell me when you two became so close?" Sarah made a sneering remark.

Clifford responded, "We're not. We're simply classmates and pals."

Sarah shrugged and said, "Well, okay." "I'm going to meet Rose right now," she continued as she walked in and gave me a brief glance.

I smirked as I said, "How good of you to come give me an escort."

Well, I was actually killing two birds with one stone when Sarah told me to walk with her here because our class wasn't starting until later, and I also called our group members to come early so we could all introduce ourselves, but I didn't have your phone number, so I agreed to walk with Sarah to come get you so we could all meet in class early. SAMUEL clarified.

Okay, that's great.

"Can we get started?" I inquired, and he replied with a nod.

We arrived at class to find only two people. A boy and a girl, the latter of whom was well familiar... Wait... I believe she's the Mary girl who approached me and started babbling about Clifford.

"Sammy!" said the boy next to Mary, and Clifford waved.

"So, Bridget, these two people here, Mary and Paul, are our group mates. Mary and Paul, and this is Bridget," she says. Clifford began with a brief introduction.

Paul greeted me with a brief handshake and said, "Nice to meet you Bridget."

"It's great to meet you," I said.

"And it's great to see you again." Mary abruptly stated,

I flashed her a friendly smile and said, "Yes, it's wonderful to see you again."

"Again?" Clifford said it again, and I nodded.

"If I had to guess, he'd say no if they told him to come."

"So, how about it? Are you coming?" Clifford had inquired.

Okay, now that we've met, let's get started. Isn't it safe to say that Clifford is our group leader? " Paul was the one who inquired.

It irritated him that Clifford was abruptly chosen as the group leader. Instead of saying "group leader," I think I should say "the person they want to dump the work on."

"If Clifford can do it, why can't you?" I abruptly inquired. He burst out laughing. "Uh, because Clifford possesses all of the characteristics of a group leader."

"Are you certain?" "And what are these qualities?" you might wonder. Paul appeared irritated by my question immediately, but he only smiled.

"He is intelligent and...

Of course, the word "smart" will always come up first; I recall being the group leader in secondary school and having all of the work fall on my shoulders; it was extremely inconvenient, and if they tried to choose another group leader, the teacher would object, claiming that "I'm smart and I should help my group team." It was infuriating.

"Not to be annoying, we're all smart, because if we weren't, we wouldn't be here; at the very least, we all wrote the exam, took the course we're studying now on our own merit, we know what we're doing, and knowing what you're doing with something you chose on your own merit means you're smart when it comes to that thing, so I clearly object to Clifford being our group leader based on our project." "And if Clifford isn't the leader, who will be?" I ask. Paul asked, nearly glaring at me.

It's either you, Mary, or me! I shook my head.

"It's best if you don't count me in." I grinned as Paul chuckled, "Me too." Mary shrugged, "Fine, then I'll be group leader."

They're not going to consider entrusting the job to me in the first place. Clifford might not mind handling everything himself. I may have had a problem with it in secondary school, but I wasn't able to express it. But not any longer.

"Fine, then be the group leader as long as the project is completed." Paul shrugged his shoulders.

"Exactly," says the author, "as long as we all work together to complete the assignment on time." Paul scoffed at what I said.

Clifford seemed buried in contemplation as I looked at him.

"So..." I started, and his and the others' gazes were drawn to me.

"Starting next week, we'll meet after class every day and spend maybe thirty minutes working on our project. What do you think?" I enquired.

"It appears to be refreshing." Paul shrugged his shoulders.

"It's all right," Mary added.

Clifford and I exchanged nods.

So we're all good with this, which is wonderful; now we just need to figure out where we'll meet. But first, I need your phone numbers in case any of you decide to cancel. " Paul grinned as I stated.

"You're sort of smart," Paul said. "I see you're a ditcher," I mocked as I reached for my phone.

"I don't think I'll be able to show off my ditching abilities with somebody like you as the group leader," Paul said as he took my phone from me.

That's why he wanted Clifford to be the group leader, so he could ignore the other members of the group while still receiving full credit for the project. Clifford has no idea he's being gullible.

I said with a smile, "I'm glad you're seeing me the way I want you to see me."

I took Paul's phone and gave it to Mary, who typed down her number, and then I gave it to Clifford.

Clifford and I sat next to each other in class, and the lecturer's voice sounded as if he had recently fought a lion.

Class was over before I knew it, and the next class had already begun and ended.

"I'm so glad tomorrow is Saturday," I exclaimed as Clifford and I exited the building.

Clifford smiled and said, "Yes, me too." He abruptly remarked, "And thank you for being the group leader."

I took a breather. "Can you tell me why you're thanking me?" I enquired.

Clifford stated, "I really didn't want to be the group leader, but I... I didn't know how to turn them down." I grinned.

I said, "Repeat after me."

He looked perplexed at me. "No way! I'm not interested in being the group's leader. Little by little, I said.

Clifford grinned. "No, I don't want to head the group," he stated again.

"There," I said, my brows furrowed at him. He also laughed.

What a sweetie

"You're something else, Bridget," Clifford said, "but it's not simple to say because their reaction will make you feel bad." I clicked my tongue and shook my head.

We both resumed our stroll, and he inquired.

"What are your plans for tonight?" I enquired.

"Nothing," I shrugged, "I'll probably simply spend the night sleeping."

What is it that he is inquiring about? "Come to the party," he suggested, "but wait." You stated that you would not attend again because I had already informed George of your problems. Why are you still on your way? " "It's difficult when you have pals like George and Sarah," I said, and he shrugged. And, if I had to guess, he wouldn't be able to refuse them if they invited him. "So, how about it? Are you coming?" Clifford enquired. "It's difficult when you have pals like George and Sarah," he shrugged. And he wasn't able to.